PRIMARY READERS
PRE-FLYERS

Mystery Island

Julie Davies
Illustrator: Gemma Hastilow

Later that morning, Star, Avril and Leo are in the village café *Tea and Books*. It is the first day of their holidays in Polcastle. They are talking about their plans.

After lunch, Star goes down to the beach to play. She loves stories. She's got a lot of imagination…

Suddenly, Star sees an old man in front of her.

5

The old man shows Star a beautiful old telescope…

Star looks at the sea through the telescope. She is very surprised!

But there *isn't* an island in the sea! The old man is very happy. Why?

t is starting to rain. Star runs back to Polcastle village.

In the café, *Tea and Books*, Star tells her friends about the telescope and the island she saw in the sea.

There *is* an old story of an island...

...and in the Middle Ages there *was* a castle...

Later that afternoon, they leave Polcastle village.
They find the castle, but there is no door in the wall.

They wait for the sun.

They follow a dark passageway under the castle, down and down, past the dungeons, until... oh, no!

Star looks through the telescope again.

They wait for low tide. The sea goes out, and…

The people tell the children about the invisible island. In the Middle Ages, Lord Polidoor lived in the castle. He was a magician.

But there is a problem. Someone wants to destroy the castle...

The children want to help, but how…? The people give the children some special presents…

The children go back up through the passageway under the castle. They come out of the door, and they hear somebody talking. They hide behind some bushes.

Oh, no!

The children are in the magician's tower. How can they escape?

The children escape from the tower, down the steps, but…

Star's sword is very special.

Well done, Star!

The children escape. They run back to Polcastle village. They go to the café. They tell Jenny about the man at the castle and his plans.

They meet the police at the hotel.

The next day, they go to the castle. Avril is reading her special book…

Evening is coming to Polcastle village. On the beach, Star looks through the telescope once more. The people on the island are happy.

Picture Dictionary

compass · destroy · island · low tide

magician · mist · passageway · pouring rain

push · steps · surprised · sword

telescope · torch · tower